CCSS Genre Realistic Fi

Essential Question
What motivates you to accomplish a goal?

Clearing the JUNGLE

by Vivienne Joseph
illustrated by Roger Harvey

Chapter 1

A JUNGLE?

Ethan galloped down the hall into the kitchen. "Hi, Mom, I'm home!" he called. He signed to her as well, because Mom was hearing impaired.

"Hi, honey." She put a carton of milk on the table. "There's something I'd like you to do today."

Ethan poured himself a large glass of milk and bit into the peanut butter and jelly sandwich she'd made him. "What's that?"

"Well, first do your homework, and then could you start cleaning up your room?"

"What's the problem with my room?"

"Oh, Ethan, it's getting more and more like a jungle every day. It's a wonder that jungle animals don't live in there with you."

Ethan took another bite of his sandwich. "I know there are piles of stuff lying around," he said, "but I'm sure there aren't any live animals."

"The trouble is," he thought, "the jungle just keeps on growing."

Ethan was proud of the sign he'd made for his door: WILD ANIMALS—PROCEED WITH CAUTION! Under the sign, he had glued his favorite photograph of a tiger roaring, showing its teeth.

He opened the door and looked around. Books and papers covered the desk, and runaway socks peeked out from underneath his bed.

His mom said his room was like a jungle, but wasn't he a brave, jungle-exploring kid? And Ethan knew where everything was—well, mostly.

Ethan moved some papers aside, opened his schoolbag, and flipped through the jumble of books and papers. He sighed and hauled everything out, suddenly remembering the book presentation that was due, which reminded him of the library book he'd borrowed. It must be due by now, but where was it?

Ethan peered under his bed. Past experience had taught him that most things ended up there.

Like a snake, Ethan wriggled under the bed on his stomach. Apart from dust bunnies, the floor was clear, and he was just crawling out when his older brother, Joe, looked in.

"Hi, how's the homework going?"

"Great! I'm on it," Ethan replied.

Joe grinned and said, "I'll be in my room if you need any help."

Ethan looked around and sighed, knowing there was only one other place the library book could be. He took a deep breath and slowly opened the door to his closet. "Watch out," he told himself. "It's dark in here."

Suddenly a stack of board games crashed down from the top shelf.

"Lucky I ducked," Ethan thought as he picked up the games. Then he noticed something in the corner of his closet—his library book! "Yes!" he said, but his relief quickly vanished when he saw that it was weeks overdue.

STOP AND CHECK

Why is Ethan's room like a jungle?

Chapter 2

I'M REALLY SORRY

"This is good," Ethan's mom said to him the next morning as he practiced his presentation.

"I've finally memorized it," Ethan replied, gathering his papers.

"You can return your library book after school." Then his mom's expression changed to shock as she caught sight of the due date. "This book is incredibly overdue! You'll have a hefty fine to pay."

Ethan swallowed and said, "Sorry, Mom, it kind of went missing in the closet."

She said, "Ethan, you can't keep making these excuses! You need to take responsibility for organizing your room."

When he arrived at school, Ethan caught up with his friends, Blake and Luis. "Did you remember your part of our science project?" Blake asked.

"I thought that wasn't due until next week," Ethan replied.

"No, it's due today," said Blake.

Luis sighed and said, "We're in trouble. Mr. Wong doesn't accept late projects."

"I'm sorry—you should've texted me," said Ethan.

Blake shrugged. "I wish I had now, but it's not my fault you forgot."

The three friends went to see Mr. Wong.

"I'm really sorry, Mr. Wong. It's my fault that we haven't finished the project," Ethan admitted.

Mr. Wong gave Ethan a serious look. "I know you're sorry, but you can do better," he said.

Ethan felt a blush creep over his face.

"Now that you are heading toward middle school, Ethan," Mr. Wong continued, "you'll need to stay organized, or you will quickly fall behind."

After class, Ethan asked Luis, "We have a book presentation due, right?"

Luis raised his eyebrows. "That's not until next week."

"I was just checking," Ethan said.

Later in the day, Mr. Wong asked Ethan for his permission slip for the field trip.

"Sorry, I don't have it with me right now, Mr. Wong, but I'm sure it's at home somewhere. I just have to find it," Ethan blurted out.

Mr. Wong looked at him crossly. "You have until tomorrow morning to hand it in, or you won't be joining us on the field trip."

Ethan was starting to feel sick to his stomach. Nothing was going right. "Things are so bad, I don't even know where to start," he thought.

After school, Ethan trudged off with Blake to catch the bus.

"I'll text you tonight to remind you about the permission slip if you want me to," Blake said.

"Okay, thanks," Ethan replied. He didn't think he'd forget, but first he had to track it down. It must be in his room somewhere.

"Want to come to my house?" Blake asked. "We can go skateboarding."

Ethan wanted to go, but then he thought about the unfinished project and the permission slip lost in the jungle of his room. "I can't today," he said, "but maybe you can come over tomorrow?"

"Tomorrow should be okay, but remember that we've got practice straight after school. You've got that in your planner, haven't you?"

Ethan didn't say anything. He hadn't seen his planner for a while and had no idea where it was.

STOP AND CHECK

What events make Ethan realize he needs to get better organized?

Chapter 3

ON SAFARI

"I've made us a snack," Ethan's mom said when he arrived home. "How did your book presentation go?"

"Wow, muffins," Ethan said, grabbing one and biting into it, filling his mouth so that he couldn't reply.

When he'd finished eating, Ethan carried his plate over to the counter and headed to his room.

"Oh, Ethan, give me that library book, and I'll renew it for you tomorrow," his mom said. "You can pay the fine out of your allowance."

"Okay," he called as he shuffled to his bedroom and dumped his schoolbag on the desk. "It isn't okay," he thought. "Nothing is okay."

He looked around, thinking about the missing permission slip, his planner, the overdue library book, and the massive library fine.

"It's all too hard," Ethan thought as he slumped onto his bed. "The jungle is winning."

"Hey, little brother." Joe poked his head in the doorway. "What's the matter?"

Ethan waved his arm around the room in reply. "It's all this ... this jungle of stuff everywhere."

Joe looked at the clutter. "What you need," he said, "is organization."

"I don't know anything about organization!" Ethan wailed.

Joe beat his chest like Tarzan. "Big brother help little brother!"

After they stopped laughing, Joe found a piece of paper and a pen. "I'll help you get started." He wrote a list. "Goal: To get organized. Step one: Clean room. Step two: Make list of what needs to be done. Step three: Write dates in planner. Step four: Write schedule and pin it to bulletin board."

Joe smiled when he finished. "I know it seems a bit ambitious, but I'm sure you can do it."

"Cleaning up this mess is tons of work." Ethan took a deep breath. "Would you help me?"

"Sorry, pal, I'm heading out for a bike ride," Joe said, patting Ethan on the back as he left.

Ethan sat for a while, thinking about the famous explorers who set off on safari through wild jungles. "I can do it," he said aloud.

He'd made a good start by the time his mom came to see how he was doing.

"Oh, my!" she said. "You're doing such a good job here. Do you want some help?"

Together they emptied out the closet. "What's this?" his mom asked, peering at a sheet of paper. "It looks like a permission slip of some kind."

STOP AND CHECK

How did Joe help Ethan?

Chapter 4

BREAKING FREE!

The next morning, Ethan gazed around his bedroom with satisfaction. It was no longer a jungle. His books were stacked neatly in the bookcase, the computer sat proudly in the middle of his desk, and beside it were his planner and a cup with all his pencils and pens. His things weren't falling out of the closet anymore either.

On the wall by the window, Ethan had pinned his calendar to the bulletin board. He had also entered all the important dates in his planner.

Today he had practice after school. He opened the closet and took out his backpack, knowing that everything he needed was already packed.

"It took a lot of determination to tame the jungle," he thought, "and it was hard work, but it was definitely worthwhile."

Blake and Luis were already waiting for him when he got to the bus stop.

"Sorry, I forgot to text you to remind you about the permission slip," Blake said.

"It's okay," grinned Ethan. He pulled the slip out of his bag.

At school, Mr. Wong announced another group project. "I'm not making new groups this time," he said. "Just stay in the same groups as before."

Ethan saw Blake and Luis look at each other and wondered if they were wishing he weren't in their group. "That's okay," he thought. "They don't realize how organized I am now."

"We'll brainstorm some ideas on the board," Mr. Wong said. "Who has a project suggestion?"

Ethan raised his hand, feeling as brave as an explorer plunging into the jungle.

Later that day when Mr. Wong asked for volunteers to do their book presentations, Ethan's hand shot into the air. "This is much better organization, Ethan," Mr. Wong remarked, smiling.

After practice, Blake and Luis came over.

"We're going out to the tree house," Ethan told his mom.

"In that case, you'd better take provisions." She put a lid on a container of sliced apples and bananas and handed it to him. "It's a real jungle out there!" she added, laughing.

It had been a long time since Ethan had played in the tree house, and the branches, covered with new growth, had closed in around it. As the boys looked up at it, the wind moved through the leaves, making it look as if an animal were stalking through the limbs. Ethan shuddered as, just for a moment, he thought he saw the eyes of a tiger looking out at them.

Ethan took a breath. "Let's go!" he said, and they all charged off into the jungle.

STOP AND CHECK

What are some of the things that show how Ethan has changed?

Respond to Reading

Summarize

Use key details from *Clearing the Jungle* to summarize what motivated Ethan to get organized. Your graphic organizer may help you.

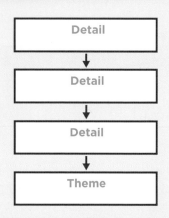

Text Evidence

1. How can you tell that *Clearing the Jungle* is realistic fiction? Use details from the text to explain your answer. GENRE

2. What is the theme of *Clearing the Jungle*? How do Joe's actions on pages 10 and 11 help communicate the theme? THEME

3. What is the meaning of *slip* on page 7? What is another meaning for *slip*? What clue helped you decide its meaning on this page? HOMOGRAPHS

4. Ethan's friends and teacher respond differently to him in Chapter 4. Write about how this change supports the story's theme.
   WRITE ABOUT READING

Compare Texts
Read about a girl who sets a challenging goal.

Just for Once

My goal is simple. My goal is achievable.

It concerns running
It concerns running

and just for once—not coming in last.
Again.
My friends help me practice,
my mom helps me, too.
"Why don't you get up earlier?" she says,
"and I'll run with you."

So I make myself wake up—
before the sun throws back the covers
of the night and shines upon our world.
It doesn't seem like fun.

My mind tells my body,
"Give up now. It's not worth all this.
You'll never improve."

But even though my legs cry
even though my legs cry,

I keep on!
I keep on!

We run together. Mom breathes hard beside me.
I'm breathing hard, too,
and the wind's breath is on my face.
The lazy sun's rising at our backs, and suddenly
my legs stop cry-baby crying,
my feet search out the ground ahead.

Every day I run, sometimes with Mom,
sometimes with Jada, Leslie, and Jordan at school.
Never with my brother, who's far too cool
to run with his kid sister, who is always last.

Soon the day of the race arrives. Am I ready?

We line up, and there's the start.
My heart pumps, my legs pump,
my mind sings my running song—

    Run well, run strong!
    Run well, run strong!

Illustration: Steve Templer

My mom calls, "Go girl, go!"
I can hear Jordan, Leslie, and Jada yell, too,
as I take off down the course.

In a flash, like lightning, like lightning,
I dash past Megan, past Trina, and Alice,
and others too!

  Is this really me?
Will this speed, this energy, last?
  Is this really me?
How long will I keep on
running this fast?

But I'm not past Caitlin, or Leanne—
they run so fast they almost fly—
they run, shoulders high.

Leanne breaks the tape, Caitlin
comes second. Guess what? I bet
no one would ever guess this—
I'm third for the very first time!
And, *at last*, most definitely,
positively,

NOT LAST!

Illustration: Steve Templer

Make Connections

How important is it for an athlete, such as a runner,
to set a goal? ESSENTIAL QUESTION

Family and friends help the main characters achieve
their goals in each story. Compare the ways they help
the runner and Ethan. TEXT TO TEXT

Focus on Literary Elements

Rhyme and Repetition Not all poems have to rhyme, and rhymes do not have to come at the ends of lines. Free verse poems don't use a regular rhyming pattern. However, poets sometimes use internal rhymes to give a rhythm to the poem. Poets can also use repetition to bring out an important idea.

Read and Find In *Just for Once*, the poet uses repetition of phrases, such as in lines 2 and 3: *"It concerns running,"* and in lines 18 and 19: *"I keep on!"* She also includes rhymes. Some rhymes are at the ends of lines, as in lines 7 and 9: *too, you.* Some rhymes are internal, as in line 10: *make, wake.* Look for more examples of both repetition and rhymes.

Your Turn

Have fun with rhyme and repetition by writing a short poem of no more than 25 words. Make at least two words rhyme, and repeat at least one word or phrase. Your poem also needs to make sense and convey an idea, a thought, a description, or a feeling. Share your poem with the class.